EVOLVE WITH ME

By:
Romane Wilson

Evolve With Me

Copyright © 2024 Romane Wilson

All rights reserved. This book or any portion thereof may not be reproduced, distributed, or transmitted in any form or by any means, including photocopying, recording, or other electronic or mechanical methods, without the expressed written permission of the publisher, except in the case of brief quotations embodied in critical reviews and certain other noncommercial uses permitted by copyright law. For permission requests, write to the publisher, addressed "Attention: Permissions Coordinator," at the address below.

Book cover image by Danielea Grant
Editing and Formatting by Tiffany Moore
Self-publish through Amazon.
First printing edition 2024

TABLE OF CONTENTS

CHAPTER 1: THE ARREST……………….……..1

CHAPTER 2: THE HOLE…………...…………...9

CHAPTER 3: GENERAL POPULATION…………18

CHAPTER 4: CHURCH…………………….....….53

CHAPTER 5: EVOLVE…………………………61

Chapter 1:

The Arrest

"It was never a lesson to be taught.
It was a lesson to be experienced."

- Tiffany Moore

Chapter 1

The Arrest

It was a very cold day on Cape Cod, Massachusetts; a typical winter day in January. I reckon it was one of those days where you would be at home watching a nice movie, under a cozy blanket. Unfortunately, that was not the case for me. I was walking down Hyannis Street puzzled and furious.

I had just got off work and discovered that the police wrongfully towed my Dodge Ram truck. Quite frankly, I always make sure to park my vehicle in a permitted parking spot. However, there I was walking to my friend's house so he could take me to the police station so I could figure out what was going on.

When I called to inquire about my car, I was told it was towed because I was being investigated. In addition to that, I had a loud muffler which they had told me to replace but I never did. I still didn't think that was a good enough reason to tow my truck. On my way to my friend's house, a police car drove past me, and I saw the police officer staring at me intensely, but I ignored him and continued walking.

Then suddenly I heard tires screeching against the road. The police vigorously turned around, approached me, and turned his blue lights on. He started to interrogate me, asking where I was headed and why I had a machete in my hand. Now that I am looking back at this day, that was not a good look at all.

Unintentionally, it appeared as if I was about to do something malicious with a machete in my hand. However, I had a machete in my hand because I used it at work that day. I am the owner of a landscaping business, Best Touch Landscape and Gardening LLC.

That day I just happened to use a machete. I told him why I had the machete in my hand, that my truck was towed, and I needed a ride to the police station. He asked me for my name after which he went into his vehicle to obtain information. A couple minutes later, I realized that two more patrol cars pulled up. The police officer approached me demanding that I conceal the machete and suggested that I put it in my backpack.

While I was putting the machete away, he mentioned that I had two warrants out for my arrest. I was very shocked! I was unaware of this and thought that the day could not get any worse. Consequently, he asked to search me. He took the machete and a knife I had in my pocket and did a complete search.

After the search, he handcuffed me and placed me in the back of the police jeep. The previous night I partied with friends. I had a great time not knowing that the next day was going to be one of the worst days of my life. I was not nervous about being brought to the police station. I just wanted to know what the warrants were about.

They brought me to the Barnstable Police Station for booking. During my search at the station, they found an empty handgun in my backpack and one bullet in my pocket. I was very surprised that the first police officer didn't find them when he did his complete search.

Immediately after that the booking officer read me my rights, took the evidence, and placed me in a cell. At that point I was like, "Why Father? Why? On a weekend? Father God, why?" This was very heartbreaking. I started to think about my business and my family. The only thing that was left for me to do that day was to burst out into tears, but I held it together and hoped for the best.

They told me that my bail was $5000, but I couldn't bail myself. I ended up spending the whole weekend in the station jail. On Monday I went to court where I was arraigned (put on trial).

No one showed up to court that day, so I was sent to the Barnstable corrections sheriff office. That is when things started to go downhill.

Chapter 2

The Hole

"When I write, I release all the pain I have built up inside."

- Tiffany Moore

Chapter 2

The Hole

After checking into the jail, I was sent to the hole. This is the worst place you could be in jail. The hole is not exactly a "hole," it's just a cell block where inmates are treated like animals. Honestly, it felt like hell on earth, it might as well have been an actual hole. This is a 24-hour lockdown everyday. I did not even get to shower which is why I said I was treated like an animal.

It was such an inhumane experience. I did not see any other inmates, only the officers that came to bring me food. I could not believe I was in such a gruesome solitary confinement situation. I did not feel like I deserved that at all.

I didn't eat for 3 days in the beginning because I did not have an appetite. I was so depressed and overwhelmed. The hole was a very brutal place! The officers would just come to my cell door to give me food. They obviously didn't really care about my well-being.

I kept on asking them why I was not in the general population (gen pop), but the officers were very rude to me and hesitant to respond. It was on the 5th day. I felt like God sent me an angel. An officer came up to my door and asked me why I was not eating and asked me why I was in the hole.

I told him I did not know why I was there, and he told me that the rest of the officers were planning to put me in the turtle suit. To my understanding, you only get a turtle suit in jail if they think you are capable of hurting yourself and others. You would think that I tried to murder someone the way they were treating me.

Eventually I found out that it was because I refused to take a shot when I checked in. No one told me if I did not take a shot they would throw me in the hole. I was just brought there. If I had known that would have been the case, I would have just taken the shot. That hole was horrendous!

That officer called for some food and told me I needed to eat. I asked him for pen and paper, and he told me that I needed to fill out a request form to get out of the hole. He gave me the ink part of a pen and a few request papers. I wasn't allowed to have an actual pen because it was considered a weapon in jail.

Once I got ink and paper, I started documenting my experience on the back of some of the request forms. Since I was going through so much, I thought I needed to put it on paper. I sent out the request forms to be placed in the general population and hoped for the best. I did not have much time with that officer because they rotated the officers every 2 hours. That officer helped to build my confidence and relieved some stress. This is why I said it felt like God sent me an angel.

Thanks to that encounter with the officer, I started eating 3 meals a day. He explained to me that if I didn't cooperate and eat my meals, they would never let me out of the hole. That is when I started to request for everyone; the doctor, the pastor, the therapist, the jail lawyer, literally everyone that was available to me. I really wanted to talk about my first 5 days in the hole.

No one knew where I was, so I wanted to see everyone to explain my situation.
I was super nice to the officer that replaced him. He told me that he saw my requests and that I would be transferred to gen pop soon. I was so excited and started talking about church. I felt comfortable talking to him. I even mentioned that I had a business and 3 children I needed to attend to.

Evolve With Me

On my 6th day in the hole, a doctor and a psychologist came to talk to me. I guess they were wondering if I was "okay in the head." He gave me a paper to fill out so I could go into the general population. He brought me to see my lawyer and got me a tablet so I could call friends and family.

After we spoke for over an hour, they told me that I would be out of there by the next day, but I will need to be on medication and see a therapist. I told them I would do anything to get out the hole and to avoid the turtle suit. Six days in the hole! I was pissed! I was furious! I was there singing songs, sleeping, barely eating, and repeating the cycle each day like a broken record.

I only got to speak to my family, but I was incredibly grateful for the calls. Unfortunately, I could not sleep on the sixth night because I was very anxious.

Chapter 3

General Population

"I made it through my nightmares.

It's time for my dreams."

- Tiffany Moore

Chapter 3

General Population

On the 7th day after breakfast, I was transferred to a general population cell, A-pod to be exact. A-pod is technically for inmates that are mentally ill or drug addicts. I did not really care about that stigma; I was just grateful to be out of the hole. I was automatically placed there because I was transferring from the hole.

Upon my arrival to A-pod, I got a tablet for my personal use, access to a ball court, and all the regular stuff. I thanked God because I was praying to get some answers and to be around other inmates. Being locked up like that can drive anyone insane. Thank God I avoided the turtle suit!

Journal entry:

It's my 10th day here and I am working out, meeting people, and filling out more paperwork to go to church. I relentlessly send out the same request forms so that they can see how serious I am. The jail lawyer came by with a run down of my charges, the weapon, the ammunition, and conspiracy. It was scary! He told me that since my charges were serious, I would definitely be doing some time. That was a very sentimental conversation. I had just started my landscaping business a few months ago and now I am feeling very remorseful.

I was in a cell by myself, and I had a lot of time to think. It was also on my 10th day that I was in my cell and the title, 'Evolve With Me' came to mind for the name of this book. I knew that after this experience I would not be the same man. I was very grateful that I wasn't in the hole anymore, where they tried to drive me insane.

I really think that was their motive. I started making calls to family to get things arranged while I prepared for my next court day in 20 days. I spent my days working out a lot since I was now on a 21-hour lockdown. We had 4 hours total of free time (wreck time).

I ate and stayed hydrated as much as I could. These were some of the things I could control. The less I worried and took care of myself, the better it was for me. Everyone was trying to talk to me while I
tried to stay to myself.

It was ironic that I wanted to be in gen pop and when I got there, I was reluctant to speak to other inmates. I just wanted to see other people. I got accepted into the church which was fun and uplifting. It kept me occupied and there were some interesting topics.

Being in jail with no money or having no one to call on the outside will make you feel like a zombie. Literally just existing with no purpose or sense of meaningfulness. As the days went by, I tried to watch the weather through my
window.

Whenever I peeked through my window I could not see outside clearly because it snowed almost everyday. Maybe if I could see some sunshine that would have made me feel a little bit better. The weather was as gloomy as my experience.

Journal entry:

I have been in for 15 days now and it really feels like 15 years. I did end up talking to some inmates and I would also listen to them while they talked to each other. It seems like they love it here. Most of them are homeless, hopeless, and do not have a job so they see jail as an opportunity to get taken care of.

When we are not on lockdown they laugh, gossip, and it appears as if they are having a wonderful time. I presume they come here every winter purposely to have a good time, then try to make it out by summer. Some of them have been coming to jail back-to-back for years. They have their jail family that they have created bonds with.

One day I was on the tablet talking to a friend and the alleged bully for the block approached me. He asked me where I was from and so forth, but I ignored him. I did not utter a word to him. He told me his name and said other things, but I just looked him in his eyes and continued to talk on the tablet. I wasn't afraid of him, but I also didn't want to be in any altercations.

I really didn't go to a place like jail to make friends either. He was a huge man with tattoos all over his face. It seemed like everyone in that pod knew him and they all gave him food. I wasn't trying to be disrespectful, but I wasn't going to talk to him. He walked off and shook his head.

Journal entry:

Everyday in jail is like a test. A pop quiz would be a better analogy. You just never know when you will be tested. You also do not want to be seen talking to the wrong person here for multiple reasons. They might wrongfully associate you and this is one of the reasons why I just want to stay to myself.

It is Friday morning and my 16th day being locked up. One of the officers came to wake me up for breakfast but for some reason, I never heard the cell open. The longer I am here, the more I am getting acclimated and a bit comfortable. I hate that but it is the sad truth. I now see how many people go to jail and become complacent and careless about life and their future. I must fight the feeling of becoming complacent daily. There is more to life than this.

Evolve With Me

It was approximately 5:30 am and everyone was already out eating on my reck. I peeked out the window to see if the sun was out, but it was snowing as usual. I went downstairs to eat my meal which was two hot dogs, and something that appeared to be mash potatoes with a few different vegetables. I can barely identify most of the food here. However, I was thankful to have something to eat.

Ever since I got here, I never stopped praying. I have literally been praying without ceasing. I pray mornings, evenings, and nights. All the things I never did on the outside, I find time to do it while locked up. Breakfast is normally like 15-20 minutes.

After that it is back to being locked down until around 10:30 am. We get one hour free to play ball, exercise, shower or whatever we want to do. We play games like dominoes, cards, or chest. I used most of my free time to shower and cut my hair.

After the 2 hours of free time, I would just go back in for another 2 hours of sleep or read a book then it would be lunch time. I had barbecue burgers that day. I never drank the juice they provided from the cafeteria. I heard too many rumors about it being unsafe to drink.

That day I was able to buy my own snacks and juice, so I drank my own. My mother and mother- in- law ensured I had money on my books. I bought lotion, toothpaste, 50 ramen noodles, sausage and a bunch of other snacks that would be enough to last until my next court date.

They say you always know who your real friends are when you are down on your face. Being in jail really showed me who really cared about me. Family is all I got at this point. Some of my friends are like my family.

When you are in a place like this, your family must really love you to pick up the phone to have a conversation, not to mention to put money on your books. I am grateful that my family did not neglect me. A lot of inmates could not say the same.

The following night at 7:30 pm I had rice and an unidentified meat. Crazy right? Thankfully, it tasted decent. I had it with two slices of cornbread. I still ate the jail food even though I had my own food. I just acted normal the whole time. I did not want to seem cocky or act like I was better than anyone. This prevented any unnecessary attention.

It was a blessing to have my own little canteen in my cell. I had food all night until

I fell asleep. I would make the famous noodles with sausage and cheese which turned into rice after a while. One of my favorite meals was noodles, sausage, some cheese, and Doritos to top it off, with a little Kool aid. I was used to my tasty Jamaican meals cooked to perfection. But I made it work because I did not have a choice.

Journal entry:

We are now on day 20 and I have been repeating the same cycle. This gets mentally draining honestly. I have been going to church every other week which really helps to keep my mind relaxed and stress free. It's great to see all the brothers that know so much about God. I also enjoy learning more about the Word of God.

I am happy to know that I am not the only one that wants to change my life around. I have always been a spiritual individual but honestly when I am in trouble that is when I tend to pray more. I know that God is a merciful God, but I need to maintain a relationship with Him even through my good times. Honestly, if it wasn't for God and writing I probably would have lost my mind already. You really have to be mentally strong to stay sane here.

On the bright side, I started hearing from more people on the outside. I am ready to be out of here. I get so emotional here thinking about my children and all the wrongs I have done. I really miss my kids; Joshua, my youngest, Cherish, my second oldest and Rahkaylia, my oldest. My children are 10, 7, and 4 years old. They really need their father.

I felt very guilty about being away from them. I promised myself that I will keep praying when I get out and not only try to have a relationship with God in times of trouble. I do believe that God allows certain things to happen in our lives so that he can get our attention. Sometimes He also wants to change our lives around, but we must allow him to. He cannot do so when we are far from Him and don't even have the time to pray.

Journal entry:

It is another stormy day, and I miss landscaping. I miss doing what I love. Being in jail while owning a business and having 3 children to take care of really opened my eyes to see how important it is to make the right decisions in life. This is definitely not a place for me. I made up my
mind to be as positive as possible because it's just not worth it.

It's almost 9:00 am and it's about to be lunch time. Sometimes I don't even want to eat because I started feeling uncomfortable eating right around the clock. Especially because I am not working. I feel lazy and unproductive. Meanwhile my brain is doing a lot of work thinking, planning, and penning my thoughts on paper.

I went for lunch and had rice and something that looked like barbecue chicken. As soon as I got back to my cell, I called Nicole, Joshua's mom, to see if I could hear my son's voice. Surprisingly, she picked up and we spoke for 30 minutes. When I heard his voice, instantaneously I was ready to get out.

I was excited and even felt more regretful about being here. I don't belong here! She wasn't happy to get the call from jail, but I am so happy she picked up. She wanted to bail me out, but I just didn't think it was right to get her involved. I spoke to my mom today as well.

I already spoke to most of my family members; my sister and brother that live close to me. I also spoke to other relatives in Jamaica, my cousins, and my father. Some of my family made arrangements to visit and bail me, but they got busy and a bit afraid because of my charges. My mom was not scared but she did say I should sit a few more days so I can learn my lesson, which I did. I understand why she said that.

I love my mom to death, and I know she has my back through thick and thin. I have already seen so many people in here not being able to reach anyone they called because no one really wants to converse with an inmate. It's just wack! I ended up talking to my baby mothers and all 3 kids, but I could not tell my kids where I was. I had to lie, and I hated it.

Every day I spent in jail; I learned something new. I got more business ideas because I had so much time to think. At least I was using my time wisely. Other inmates got into more trouble during their free times.

Some inmates were not motivated to be or do better. I have never been a follower; I am a leader, and I know that I have a bright future ahead of me. I used the time to change my perspective on life, grow, and most importantly evolve.

Unfortunately, one day I started to feel sick. I thought I had Covid-19 because my body ached terribly, and I was very weak. I was convinced that it was Covid-19 due to the fact that I wasn't vaccinated, and it was super gross in the jail. I took a test, but it took 4 days to come back, and it was negative. I cleaned my cell like twice a day, but I still managed to get sick. I wrote a slip to see the nurse and patiently waited for them to show up.

I never had dinner that night because of how I was feeling. I just made some ramen noodles and went to bed. The medication that the nurse gave me thankfully helped and I recovered from whatever that was. As you can see, I have encountered so much while locked up in such a short period of time.

Journal entry:

Nothing much happened today. I woke up early for some breakfast then went back to bed for a couple hours. I must mention that all the things I used to rush to do on the outside, I now try to spend more time doing them. I actually lotion my whole body now, which I never used to do.

I ended up buying a sweet scent cocoa butter lotion. I am in love with it. I also got cocoa butter bar soap because I was tired of using their small soap. I also bought a better deodorant. The one they gave me was decent, but I felt like I needed a better one.

That is when I realized that I was taking better care of myself, growing spiritually, changing my perspective, developing better habits and discipline. It is through our experiences that we gain wisdom and growth. This felt like my personal bootcamp experience. These are the types of testimonials that can help other people in life so that they can overcome challenging times or encourage them to make better choices. I was excited to share my experience and be a good influence in society.

Journal entry:

It is my 19th day here and I am up early like the birds. The cell doors opened for breakfast, and I never forgot to say a prayer, especially after I started my church sessions. I normally go to church on the outside on Sundays, so I am not a stranger to God. He said to call on Him in times of trouble, but I must reiterate that being in here gave me the revelation that it is not only in times of trouble I should call on Him. I went out for breakfast after prayer and had the regular cereal.

It's a Tuesday and they repeat the same food as the previous weeks. I guess that is how jail is. Specific days are chosen for the same thing for breakfast, lunch, and dinner or chow. They call it by different names and that's another word they use. After my cereal which is normally Frosted Flakes, a box of milk, two eggs, and some extremely hard bread. Again, we get 15-20 minutes to eat.

After my reck deck is finished eating, the bottom reck deck would go out to eat. The next day they would go out to eat first then after 20 minutes, the top reck would head out. After breakfast I went to bed and slept for a few more hours until lunch time. I had rice and barbecue meat then went back to my cell where I would do my 10 push ups. This is a motivation drive to kill time as well. It helps me to push myself and keep me focused on getting out. I need to attend to my landscaping business and be a father for my kids.

My daughter, Cherish, was already asking where I was, and I ended up telling her the truth. I had a conversation with her mom the night before and she was concerned. She asked me to bring her to Ryan's World. This is one of her favorite indoor playgrounds.

I could not lie to her anymore. She is only 7 years old. I felt like it was better that she heard it from me than from someone else.

That is the type of bond I try to build with my kids. I know it is a bad place to be, but the truth is the truth. She was sad but she did not cry.

She was positive and was anxious for me to get out. She also mentioned that she was going to call the police and tell them to leave her daddy alone. That made me laugh so hard. I only have 11 more days until my court date, and I am ready to go. After my little exercise session in the jail cell, I read my bible which I got from the pastor.

If I wasn't reading the Bible, then it would be a book from the service I attended. This helped the days to go by a bit quicker.

Sometimes I get really tired and just sleep. It's getting dark, it's almost time for chow. I decided that I am going to try to talk to my oldest daughter Rahkaylia, she lives in Jamaica.

I knew it was going to be difficult to get to my baby mother in Jamaica, because it's an international call. To compromise, I just called someone here in America and had them conference the call. I did not tell her anything, I just checked up on her. I don't think she has the same mindset as cherish. Cherish is the tough one.

I did not eat the jail food that night, instead I made my own meal. I cooked with plastic bags. I heated water for the pepperoni sausage, and noodles as rice. I squeezed cheese and Doritos and made some Kool-Aid. I ended up reading about Job in the Bible that night. The book of Job is a powerful book in the Bible. This testimony teaches you how God will change your story if you have unwavering faith during your trials in life.

Job lost everything; his business, his family, even his health deteriorated. Job's entire body was infected with boils. His wife told him to curse God and die, but Job trusted in God even more. *Though he slay me, yet will I trust in him (Job 13:15).* He remained faithful to God and in the end, God restored everything and gave

him twice the blessing from before. Job and his wife had two different perspectives on the situation, and this shows how powerful your mind is.

I just kept on thinking about my business and all the money I was missing out on. I missed my kids, I missed working, and I missed my mom. She was stressed out. By then I was at a point where I hated sleeping. I had developed insomnia. I'm sure this was from all the stress.

Evolve With Me

Journal entry:

Twenty days of lockdown and it feels like 20 years. The fact that my court date is in

a few days makes me feel more positive than ever. I started my day with a word of prayer. Sometimes I don't wake up until they open the cell door for breakfast but because I am so excited to get out of here, I was already up.

I got up and walked around until it was time to eat. Normally I would wake up, spread my bunk, and walk around until the door was open. Sometimes I would do some reading, or I would just sing songs to keep myself entertained. It was the famous egg for breakfast! I do not really pass on eggs.

After breakfast it was lockdown again. I went back to the cell and brushed my teeth. I hated brushing my teeth before I ate because it took away the taste. Instead of going back to bed after breakfast I did a few push ups. Then I laid down until 9:30 am which was lunch time.

I felt bad for some people because they had nothing to eat during those two hours. They depended on breakfast, lunch, and dinner. When I cook during my free time, I would just leave it in the cell until it is time to go back in. I tried to keep my belly full because being locked in and hungry is just not it.

I never got any visits because the paperwork I filled out was still in process. However, they have this machine for video calls which makes it feel like an in person visit.

It is crazy because even if friends and family came to visit; it is not like you could touch them. There is a huge glass between you and them. The only difference between the video call and the actual visit is just the effort someone would put into coming all the way there to talk to you for 30 minutes.

Chapter 4:

Church

I was glad when they said unto me, let us go into the house of the Lord.

(Psalms 122:1 KJV)

Chapter 4

Church

Church was usually twice a week, but I wished it was more often. There would be inmates from A-pod, where I was, B-pod and C-pod. I was a little skeptical about this combination. Every inmate was placed in a pod based on their charges or other reasons that would make anyone nervous.

However, what surprised me the most was that the inmates liked to participate in the services. They would ask questions, tell their stories, and I could tell they appreciated each service as much as I did. They were surprisingly very happy while in church. It was uplifting to see everyone growing in their faith in God. We were all growing spiritually together.

I was excited to go to church every time. Firstly, I got the chance to be out of the cell during lockdown, and it was very satisfying to talk to others with the same mindset. Secondly, I was raised in a Christian home so I would have answers to some of the questions asked. I would give insightful feedback on topics discussed. It felt good to be able to participate.

I had great conversations with the other people in the church and I would always bring back a book to my cell to read. I found pleasure in learning new things and building my vocabulary. I was now in love with reading and writing. If I wasn't locked up, I wouldn't have developed such great passions for reading and writing.

One of the many things I learnt because of going to church was about Saint Moses

The Black. I read an article about how he changed his life around. Saint Moses The Black was an Ethiopian slave, who had a bad reputation of stealing and gang involvement. Learning about him really humbled me. He converted to a monk and became a very humble and calm man. He was well respected for his peaceful advice and holy council. He is a notable example of what it really means to evolve.

The fact that he was a slave and an African known to his peers as Abba Moses is interesting. I liked everything about this guy except the fact that he became a priest. This article inspired and empowered me to keep pushing. If you are not smart in jail, there is a 100 percent chance you are getting in a fight or getting into more trouble. Staying to myself and being polite was the route I chose.

The most important thing about church was that the preacher and other members of the group did not treat us like criminals. They all have a past too. Every saint has a past. They might never have been convicted but their stories showed that nobody is perfect, but we have a choice to change our trajectory. Normally it is 6 to 7 visitors coming together for the service and most

times they are all from different churches. I remember one specific
meeting; the conversations were so authentic. I was a little nervous.

No matter how you started life, you have the power in you to change your story. Although jail is not the best place to learn all these things, I do appreciate what I have learned and some of the people I met. However, I would not wish jail on my worst enemy.

It is always a great feeling to me to learn more about God and to know that because of the service we can come together. We even got the opportunity to partake in holy communion. I never ate the bread (representing God's body). We said a prayer and I watched almost everyone eat their bread, but I had a different plan for mine. I kept the bread in my Bible like a souvenir, so His body would always be with me.

Chapter 5:

Evolve

"Your life may take a detour, but your destiny will remain the same."

-Tiffany Moore

Chapter 5

Evolve

Journal entry:

Being here in jail is getting very annoying. This constant cycle, doing the same thing daily is mentally draining and so depressing. I have 5 days left until court and I am trying to stay to myself even more. I cannot do anything to get in any trouble that could result in another charge.

If that happens, I could get more time and that is the last thing I want to happen. I am currently being super nice to everyone. I am not trying to have any enemies. I do not really start conversations but I did play a few games of draft just so I did not seem antisocial. The closer I get to my court date, the more anxious I become.

I was considering starting another business which is car detailing. I want to get out and be the best that I can be in every aspect of my life. However, I decided that I would just focus on the one business for right now. It is wise to have one successful business and then an expansion can be considered. This business is only one year old, so I am just thinking about the best approach to take.

The business ideas were coming to me so quickly. But I realized that my thought process was becoming more strategic and rational. I would do anything to keep myself busy, and out of trouble once I got out. I almost got in a fight on my 25th day when the guys decided to have a cooking mix (everybody put something to cook).

That night I was going to "throw down" meaning I was going to give them a noodle, Doritos, and some pepperoni

I got all the ingredients and went over to the guys, but this man had the audacity to say to me, "We ain't cooking with you bro, you mad gay." I shook my head and just walked away to make my own meal. I can confidently say that myself control was activated.

I was proud of myself because I definitely saw the growth. In my culture that was a major offense, and I had all the right to retaliate. Many others would have acted on a comment like that thinking that they do not have anything else to lose.

I think that because I was staying to myself for so long, he was mad. He never stopped cursing me out and calling me names until this extremely muscular female correction officer came over and told him to go to his cell.

It was wreck time, when we had 2 hours of free time for ourselves. A few minutes after he was locked in, she called for backup and that's when two other male officers came in and said, "Romane, if you had said a word, you would be going back to the hole too." They arrested him, removed him from the unit, and brought him to the hole.

I felt so bad I went to my cell to eat my food and never came back out for the rest of my free time. I never intended for someone else to get in trouble either. However, that was not my fault. I hoped that was my first and hopefully my last altercation with anyone.

Journal entry:

The days are just going by, and I am having mixed emotions. It's almost my court day and I am on my best behavior. I cannot afford to mess up, even though I am tested everyday. Just when I thought I was going to be alone in my cell, I got a cellmate.
That was one of my biggest tests. Sleeping with a stranger in the same cell is not one of the things I wanted to do. He spoke three

different languages, and he had three crosses tattooed on his neck. He seemed polite at first because he did say hello to me, but the three crosses on his neck threw me off.

Although I was hesitant to even talk to him, I ended up giving him half of a honey bun and noodles because he had no snacks, and he looked hungry. I would not allow him to be hungry and I had food I could share with him. This guy was always talking on his tablet. The first day he came in he was calling everyone.

Sometimes he spoke English, Spanish, and another language I could not identify. He was always talking to someone! This was very aggravating, but I didn't let it bother me.

We went an entire day with no problem. The next day I woke up, I noticed he was giving me attitude. Then he started complaining to one of the guards that I never stopped snoring, so I reminded him, "You are always on your phone talking very loudly." After that there was a lot of tension. It is crazy because I did not go complaining about him, but he did.

I was not afraid of him. I just became more cautious because I had to sleep with this guy in the same cell for another couple of days. The next day was decent, there was no argument. I started to regret even exchanging words with this guy because he was a complainer. I did not regret sharing food with him, I just learned my lesson.

The second night we had a huge argument because I was reading my Bible aloud and for some reason it annoyed him. I wondered why. He must have had some demon in him because how does reading the Bible bother anyone? It is crazy how he felt so comfortable to be on his phone all the time. He obviously never considered me. He did not have any conscience. He told me to shut up! I was so shocked! I froze up for a few seconds then I got so pissed.

I was ready to go off on him but instead I calmly said, "You can't shut me up." I was so proud of myself because the old me would have burst out in anger and made things worse. That was very disrespectful, and it really could have ended horribly.

I continued to read while he was having a conversation on his phone in Spanish.

After reading I started to sing. I was singing for a good hour, and I could tell he was upset. But at that point I did not care because his constant conversations in different languages were confusing and annoying, but I learned how to not let it bother me.

Late in the night about 3:29 am, I heard him complaining again to a correction officer, "I can't sleep, please help me." I fell back asleep right after. I was not worried about his complaints or if he would try to hurt me in my sleep. I was top bunk, and he was on the bottom bunk, so I at least had one advantage.

That morning when I woke up, I was alone. It seemed like they had moved him out. He did not last 3 days with me. I was so happy not only because of that but I also had court in two days.

Journal entry:

I have court tomorrow!!! I am happy and nervous at the same time. I started the morning the regular way but more cautious. I did not have breakfast this morning because I knew tomorrow this time, I would be out the door for my court hearing. I just gave my tray to someone. I normally try to sit at a table by myself, but someone always ends up coming over to talk to me. I was too excited to eat at this point.

Evolve With Me

At lockdown I did not want to call anyone since I was talking to the same people every day or every other day. But I also did not want it to seem like I was burning my bridges. My dad's girlfriend, Tracey, has been talking to me almost every night. She motivated me to just behave myself and reminded that I would be out soon. My close friend, Jonelle, was an everyday thing. I would call her everyday after six when she got out of work.

I would say we talked for almost an hour everyday since my mom gave me her number. She is special to me, so I did write to her even though I was calling her everyday and she picks up the phone we share the same birthday day. I have known her for almost 7 years. I wrote her and sister, Lyria, those are the only two people I ended up writing to while locked up.

My mom did put more money on my books for the canteen, but I hate to call her daily just to hear how stressed out she was. I would call her like twice a week, but I am thankful for her and Tracey. They both put money on my book and ended up becoming friends. My mom was so upset about my charges she did not want to talk to me, but Tracey came true for me and gave her a power talk.

After a long day of barely eating and being anxious, I could not sleep knowing my court was in the morning. I already knew I had anxiety because my therapist told me, and I honestly could tell. I just watched the correction officer patrol the block every couple minutes. I stayed up until the sun came out. That morning, we got called out for breakfast and it was the good old pancakes and sausage.

I did eat that because the pancakes hit in the early mornings, with that syrup and a small box of milk. I did get an apple, but I normally give it away. Something about apples turned me off because of how Eve tricked Adam with it. I am convinced that it was an apple that she gave me. I do not know; I was just extra spiritual and overthinking. No one really refused apples in jail, so it was an easy giveaway.

After breakfast it was time to go. I went upstairs to my cell, said a prayer asking God to help me get out and to keep me on the right path so I do not end up back in the hell hole. A few minutes later after praying, my cell was open along with a few others. They called my name," Mr. Wilson, you have court."

It felt like Christmas! I had already given away all my snacks, lotion, and everything I bought in the canteen. It is a significant risk because if I do not get bail, I would have had to start all over, but fingers crossed I was exercising my faith. I knew God would answer my prayers. Everything was always a process, so I had to go through the procedure to be sent out in the wagon.

Court dates were scheduled for a few people to go at that same time so there were females getting processed as well. We would change from the jail clothes to court clothes if we had it. I had the clothes

I was arrested in, so I wasn't exactly dressed for court. I just changed from the jail clothes to the work clothes I had on that day on the 20th of January.

It is now February 20th. It was a long wait to be processed and to get changed. I would say it took about an hour. They had different wagons for different groups of inmates. It is six people max that go in the wagon. It has two different sections, three on one side and three on the other side. When my cell was opened again in the lobby, this time they cuffed me and directed me and 5 other inmates to the sheriff's minivan.

After another 15 minutes we were on the way. The wagon was a whole different experience. You cannot see where you are going. You only know when the van is moving or when it stops unless you are sitting up front where you could look through the windshields of the van.

Whoever sat upfront could see the driver and the other correction officer but there is a bar between us. The wagon was like another cell with cameras inside. I was driving for approximately 45minutes. The other inmates were chatting nonstop, and constantly asking to adjust the temperature. I was quiet the whole time while everyone was just chatting away. I could tell that it was a regular thing for them.

When I arrived at the Barnstable Court House, I felt like a free man, but I was still a bit worried after coming out the wagon cuffed. We were placed in another holding cell at the courthouse until my lawyer showed up. It was very miserable down there because everyone was anxious to find out if they were going to get out or if they were getting another court date. I was just as worried, so I started to sing aloud.

This older guy that was in the same cell with me was like, "Can you shut up?" I looked at him and said, "You can't tell me to shut up." Then I continued singing. I was like "Why is everyone always trying to shut me up?" A couple minutes later his lawyer came, and he was free, leaving me alone.

About 15 minutes later my lawyer came to see me and told me that I was not going in front of the judge and there was no one upstairs to bail me. I almost fainted! I was confused and I did not have my contact list with me. Immediately after saying that she left. I was so mad, I started singing even louder. As you can see singing is one of my coping mechanisms.

I was there lost but still hopeful. I was singing a gospel song reminding myself to be faithful and to have patience. There is just peace in your mind when you sing gospel songs. God is so real! I thought to myself that the worst thing that could have happened was that I would just go back to the jail house and get another date.

Approximately 20 minutes passed, and I was still trying my best to be patient. But I was about to lose it. Next thing I know a correction officer, from the holding cell in the courthouse, came up to me and asked me for my hands. I pushed both hands through the front of the cell door and he unlocked the cuffs.

I was thinking two things: either I was going back to the big jail, or I was going in front of the judge. He opened the cell door then took the cuffs off my feet. I still was not asking any questions, not because I was afraid or shy. I was just working with the flow. He then instructed me to walk with him and he took me upstairs.

I noticed I was not going up the stairs to go to the judge; it was another path. When I got to the top floor, a police officer came to meet me and brought me through another door. I was so excited but sad at the same time. I could not even smile.

I saw my mom sitting down crying. I was angry suddenly just by the look on my mother's face. I walked up to the clerk and signed my bail log. They told me to keep a copy, give my mom the original and they held on to a copy as well.

After that I just went straight to my mom and hugged her for a good minute. I was excited to be free, but I was very emotional. I felt sad and embarrassed. My mom was not feeling good, so I walked her to her car with my arm wrapped around her shoulder.

I did the driving because she was tired. I drove back to the jail and grabbed my phone and other belongings. I also had some money remaining on my books and they gave me the remaining balance on a card. I left the jail making a firm declaration. "This is my last time here in Jesus name."

I had to run some errands and get my tools organized. They were all over the place. My stepdad, Dwayne, gave me his car and we were driving around looking for a vehicle so I could be mobile again. It was still winter, but I had some unfinished projects that I needed to complete. Back to reality where I can enjoy my family, my business and other businesses to come.

Journal entry:

It has been an entire day since I got bail, and it felt like I just migrated from Jamaica.

It is like a fresh start, but it is not like I had spent the night at a hotel. I was ready to get back to work. I was so positive and determined. I could not just lay in bed all day because I rested for a whole month. I knew I was starting from scratch again, but I was confident that this time will be better than the last.

What was I going to tell these customers that I was in jail? I did not want to lie but I had to figure out a plausible excuse. I thought that maybe I would tell them that I was sick. I called my pastor and admitted that I was locked up because I had some things to do at her house and the church. Miss Janice was so nice; I just could not lie to her. (I found it hard to lie for the most part, as you can see). She understood and said, "Romane, I forgive you, stop by when you can."

The day was already done, and I had so much to do. I was anxious and ready because success was calling my name. I did not want to be in a big rush either. I wanted to be patient and get things done right. My new motto was I wanted to move slowly with precision so I can live long like a turtle.

I admire turtles and that motto meant a lot to me. I would advise everyone to be humble, be kind to each other because violence does not pay. Jail is not a bed of roses; it is not a walk in the park. Stay away from trouble as my grandmother Mel would say, "Walk far from trouble."

I knew everything was going to be fine. I have always been a resilient person. I just need to remain focused, keep the same energy I had in jail, and pray everyday. I made a vow to myself and God that I would never go back to jail. I have too much potential within me. We all make mistakes at times, but it is what we do after those mistakes that really count.

Will you rise and look at every new day as another chance to grow, live, and evolve?

Everybody deserves a second chance but make sure that when you get the second chance you make the best of it. Will you forget about the things in the past and walk boldly into your next chapter? There is beauty in the ashes, and I am grateful that I can be a witness to this.

I wrote a whole book! Writing a book requires a lot of determination, consistency, and patience. This process showed me that I have great qualities within me, and I can do anything I put my mind to. With God all things are possible.

My business is progressing, my children are happy and well taken care of, I am staying out of trouble, and most importantly I am able to use my story to be a testament to what it really means to evolve. This book will also be a constant reminder that my worst days are behind me and better days are ahead. Sometimes we must go through things in order to learn. With those experiences and lessons learned we become more grounded individuals.

I hope that you will be able to take something from this book. Life is a journey, and we should always thrive to learn, grow, and evolve. The tests and adversities will come but they help to mold us into the better versions of ourselves. Life is what you make it, and you have the power within you to make it great.

"Stop feeling sorry for yourself and start planning solutions."
-Tiffany Moore

Made in the USA
Columbia, SC
29 April 2025